The Story Of The Comte De Chambord: A Trilogy...

George Augustus Sala

Nabu Public Domain Reprints:

You are holding a reproduction of an original work published before 1923 that is in the public domain in the United States of America, and possibly other countries. You may freely copy and distribute this work as no entity (individual or corporate) has a copyright on the body of the work. This book may contain prior copyright references, and library stamps (as most of these works were scanned from library copies). These have been scanned and retained as part of the historical artifact.

This book may have occasional imperfections such as missing or blurred pages, poor pictures, errant marks, etc. that were either part of the original artifact, or were introduced by the scanning process. We believe this work is culturally important, and despite the imperfections, have elected to bring it back into print as part of our continuing commitment to the preservation of printed works worldwide. We appreciate your understanding of the imperfections in the preservation process, and hope you enjoy this valuable book.

THE STORY

OF THE

COMTE DE CHAMBORD.

THE STORY

OF THE

COMTE DE CHAMBORD:

A Trilogy.

BY

GEORGE AUGUSTUS SALA.

"O Musa, suggere mihi causas earum rerum: quo Deorum violato, vel quo scelere offensa Regina Deorum coëgerit hominem pietate illustrem agitari tot calamitatibus, et suscipere tot labores. Tantusne furor inest mentibus divinis?"

VIRGIL, ÆNEID, I.
(*Ad usum Serenissimi* DELPHINI.)

LONDON:
GEORGE ROUTLEDGE AND SONS,
THE BROADWAY, LUDGATE.
NEW YORK: 416, BROOME STREET.
1873.

(*All rights reserved.*)

FR 1645.55

HARVARD COLLEGE LIBRARY
FROM
THE BEQUEST OF
EVERT JANSEN WENDELL
1918

"The Story of the Comte de Chambord" originally appeared in the *Daily Telegraph* newspaper; and, with the permission of the Proprietors of that Journal, and with numerous alterations and additions, is now republished.

TO

𝔥𝔦𝔰 𝔍𝔪𝔭𝔢𝔯𝔦𝔞𝔩, 𝔍𝔬𝔶𝔞𝔩, 𝔬𝔯 𝔍𝔢𝔭𝔲𝔟𝔩𝔦𝔠𝔞𝔫 𝔐𝔞𝔧𝔢𝔰𝔱𝔶

TO-MORROW,

THIS BOOK

IS,

WITH THE COMPLETEST CONVICTION

OF PROFOUND IGNORANCE

AS TO WHAT THAT MORROW MAY BRING FORTH,

HOPEFULLY DEDICATED.

  Ah, Demain, c'est la grande chose !
   De quoi Demain sera-t-il fait ?
  L'homme, aujourd'hui sème la cause,
   Demain Dieu fait mûrir l'effêt.

  * * * * * * *

  C'est l'astre qui change de zone ;
   C'est Paris qui suit Babylone ;
  Demain, c'est le sapin du trône :
   Aujourd'hui c'en est le velours.

       VICTOR HUGO.

THE STORY OF THE COMTE DE CHAMBORD.

INTRODUCTORY.

SOME five-and-thirty years since—I know that it was at a period between the Coronation of Queen Victoria and the Second Funeral of Napoleon the Great: both of which occurrences are, from the fact of my having witnessed them, indelibly impressed on my memory—I was a small boy at a solemn *Pension* in Paris attached to the College Bourbon (it became subsequently the Lycée Bonaparte, and of its present designation I have not the remotest idea) in the Rue St. Lazare; whither we proceeded every morning and afternoon to repeat our lessons: returning at nightfall to our boarding-house in the Rue de Courcelles, to eat, and study, and kick one another's shins under the table, and smoke surreptitiously, and sleep, and do everything, in fine, but Play: athletic sports not being then among the relaxations of Young France. I know that, completely divorced from leap-frog and hockey as I was, and utterly alone among hundreds of strange boys who made faces at me, called me "Pomme de terre," and sometimes pinched my arms black and blue, all in consequence of the Duke of Wellington's having won the Battle of Waterloo, I felt very much like a young Job, and inclined to curse the day when the *Harlequin* Steamer, bound from St. Katherine's Wharf to Boulogne, bore me away from Old England.

I am only led to speak of the epoch and the circumstances of my education for the reason that in 1838-9 my school (every school is a microcosm) afforded a not unedifying spectacle of the political world in miniature. At least half a dozen factious parties, all furiously hostile to each other, were represented between the Classe du Sixième, in which I was the last and stupidest scholar, and the Classe de Rhétorique, the highest division, and of which a bright creole-looking lad, called Alexander Dumas the Younger, was captain. Alexander *fils* was then a red-hot Orleanist, and his papa, Alexander *père*, frequently dined with MM. d'Orleans, de Némours, de Joinville, and de Montpensier. Among my own form-fellows were the two sons of Casimir Delavigne, the author of the furiously Republican *chanson* of "La Parisienne," and a nephew of Jacques Laffitte, who was Bonaparte's banker. I remember, also, a little Vicomte de Barruel, whose great-uncle, the Abbé de Barruel, a Legitimist of the Legitimists, and a Clerical of the Clericals, had written a History of the French Revolution (not forgotten by Mr. Carlyle), and in which things were made rather hot for the Girondins and the Jacobins. The Orleanist boys (then the prevailing party) used to dig the young Vicomte in the ribs with pieces of slate-pencil, twitch him by the nose, and otherwise despitefully use him; saluting him as a "Carlist," and with the supplementary epithets of "*gueux*," "*cancre*," "*pied-plat*," and other terms of endearment.

Why he should have been perpetually upbraided with the unconstitutional proceedings of Polignac and Peyronnet used (I was a very small boy) to puzzle me as much as why I should be held personally responsible for the triumph at Mont St. Jean of F.M. the Duke of Wellington.

Our *répétiteur* was an out-and-out Republican, the son of an old Deputy of the Convention, and, it was rumoured among us, that he knew a great deal more about the regicide conspiracy of Fieschi than he cared to avow. The tutor with whom we boarded and lodged was a Constitutional Royalist, and a Corporal in the National Guard. He had been a Constitutional Royalist so far back as 1789. Subsequently he had been a *Fédéré*, a Sectionary, an offiical short-hand writer to the Council of Five Hundred: he had seen Robespierre guillotined, Charles X. crowned, and the Tuileries sacked by the mob on July 29th, 1830. His wife was a Legitimist *pur sang*. From her I first heard the story of Marie Alacoque and the legend of the Sacred Heart; her little daughter, Desirée, was "*vouée au bleu*"—dedicated to the Virgin; and she used to kiss and fondle the little Viscount, and give him goodies when the boys were too hard upon him in the matter of the unconstitutional proceedings of Polignac and Peyronnet. I observed that the Constitutional Royalists and the Republicans were always most merciless in their persecutions of this unhappy young adherent of the Elder Branch. Some kindness was occasionally shown him by the two sons of a General and Count of the First Empire—a soldier who had lost two of his fingers by frostbite in the Retreat from Russia—a mischance which had not prevented him from fighting at Leipsic, at Montmirail, and at Waterloo. He had been proscribed and exiled at the Restoration; and, deprived of his pay and pension, and with nothing but the Cross of the Legion and the *mens conscia recti* to warm the cockles of his good old heart, had bravely earned his bread as a riding-master in a circus at Brussels, and as a fencing-master in London. Better times had come with the Revolution of '30, and he had returned to have his sons educated at the College Bourbon. "*Car, voyez-vous,*" he was wont to say, "*c'était autrefois le Lycée Impérial Bonaparte.*" It was to be the Lycée Bonaparte once more, and so lose its Imperial name once again. He was very kind to me (notwithstanding that unfortunate affair at Mont St. Jean), and on high days and holidays would take his boys and myself out walking; treating us imperially at the Café de la Rotonde, and taking us to the Cirque, when some grand battle-show piece, all prancing horses and gunpowder smoke, was being played. Nor did he fail, as we endeavoured to keep pace with his martial stride, to tell us brave stories of the days of old, and the long result of time. Especially would he discourse of a certain Little Corporal who wore a grey great-coat and a little cocked hat. It was the Little Corporal's hand that had first pinned the red ribbon on the General's breast. "*Et il m'a embrassé sur les deux joues—les deux joues,*" the battered old warrior would say. Then he would cry a little; but plucking up courage would encourage us to compete at that famous match on the bagatelle boards of the Champs Elysées, and in which the first prize was a plaster statuette of "Lui." They used to call the Little Corporal "Lui" in 1838-9. The Government did not encourage any discourse in public places about "L'Empereur." The name of Napoleon I. was indeed bruited about, when his ashes were brought from St. Helena, to be buried on the banks of the Seine, among that French people whom he loved so well; but as his nephew, Prince Louis Napoleon—afterwards to be Napoleon III.— happened to be just then in gaol, awaiting his trial for high treason, the praises of the Emperor which were temporarily permitted, had somewhat of a hollow sound.

Turning my back on that school-microcosm of thirty-five years since, and facing the world of politics, roaring around us now, is there, I venture to inquire, much to choose between the factious jumble of 1838-9 and that of 1873? Have many—have any steps in advance been made to solve the problem which distracted France then, as it distracts it to-day? Alexander cut the Gordian Knot; but the *nodus Gallicus* seems to be one susceptible of growing again, after being severed, and in a more complicated form than ever. The Queen, whose Coronation Procession I saw sweep down Parliament Street, lives and reigns, increasing only, year by year, the treasures of love and veneration heaped up for her out of the hearts of a free and contented people; while France :—well, France waits for the coming of the Potentate to whom I have dedicated this book. "Where are you going to dine?" asked the Bohemian's friend. "I'll tell you to-morrow," was the reply; and To-morrow France will inform us under what form of government she will consent, for a few years, for a month, a week, a day, or an hour, to live.

I do not think that this little pamphlet needs any further preface than the apologue concerning the politics of the College Bourbon which I have presumed to relate.

G. A. S.

I.

THE CHILD OF THE MIRACLE.

In the year 1816 Louis XVIII., King of France and Navarre, for the second time restored, after an exile of more than five-and-twenty years, to the throne of his ancestors, began to be somewhat disquieted in his mind as to the perpetuation of the Bourbon line. He himself was old, infirm, and childless; but his brother and designated successor, the Comte d'Artois, had two sons. The first was the Duc d'Angoulême, a sickly, silent, morose man, married to a princess, not indeed morose, but as silent and more sorrowful than her lord—Marie Thérèse de France, indeed, the daughter of Louis XVI., the "Orphan of the Temple." Her childhood had been passed in the stately Palace of Versailles; her girlhood in the horrible gaol of the Temple—released from which, she had wandered about for years in a restless, memory-haunted banishment; coming back to France in 1814, a bride, it is true, but an utterly crushed and disconsolate woman. Her father and mother had been torn from her arms to be dragged to the scaffold; her brother, the Dauphin, had been beaten and starved to death almost beneath her eyes; she had wanted food, raiment, light even, in her foul dungeon; and, when prosperity came, it was too late, for the heart of Marie Thérèse de France was dead within her. So the Duc and Duchess d'Angoulême were solemn couple, and, in 1816, were childless.

The second son of the Comte d'Artois was Charles Ferdinand, Duc de Berri. Those who knew this youthful Prince were wont to say that his worth lay more in his heart than in his appearance; since he was stunted in stature, broad-shouldered, beetle-browed, shaggy-haired, with a *nez camus*, thick lips, and "something of a wild and ferocious expression." An English nobleman who met him, following in the wake of the Allied Armies in '14, described the Duke as being coarse and well-nigh brutal in his manners; giving himself all the airs of a *sabreur*, without having done anything to warrant the assumption of martial roughness. He was fond, after the Restoration, of mingling with the old soldiers of

Napoleon, and inciting them to fight all their battles o'er again, and tell how fields were won, over a *chopine* of wine; but the *vieux grognards* rather mistrusted this blustering Kite, who had taken up his quarters in the Eagle's nest; and did not half like being hail-fellow-well-met with a general whose "baptism of powder" had been of the scantiest. It would seem, however, that the Duc de Berri was very much belied, and that he was, in reality, not at all a bad sort of Prince. He was, those who knew, loved, and understood him, declared, "constant in love, firm in friendship, eager for action, and ambitious for glory,"—which it could scarcely be considered his fault if he did not acquire on the field of battle; since between 1815 and 1820 there was no glory worth mentioning procurable by Frenchmen. That military promenade into Spain in 1822, which culminated at the Trocadero, yielded, truly, a few shrivelled and weedy laurels; but they were gathered by Charles Ferdinand's melancholy and taciturn brother, the Duc d'Angoulême.

Thus, though two kinsmen, his father and his elder brother, stood between him and the throne, the Duc de Berri was not only the possible and probable, but the humanly certain Dauphin of a very few years to come. His sarcastic, Epicurean uncle, King Louis, was now very old, and gross and feeble. His father, the Comte d'Artois, was a dried-up, lugubrious, self-mortifying Prince, who was atoning for a youth of profligacy by elderly asceticism of a very grim and uncomfortable nature.

"Monseigneur faisait son salut," devout Legitimists said; and "Monseigneur" seemed to be bent on working out his lasting salvation by making himself as wretched on earth as ever he possibly could. He had lost many years before, in England, and by a terrible malady, a mistress—she was somebody else's wife— whom he passionately loved; and that melancholy event, so the less devout but more scandal-loving Legitimists averred, had first caused "Monseigneur" to see the error of his ways. Lastly, there was the brooding, umbrageous Angoulême, who, it was certain, cared very little about becoming Dauphin, and less about being Louis XIX.

Charles Ferdinand, Duc de Berri, was thus the hope of the Bourbon race.

There was, to be sure, a *branche cadette*, a junior stem. There was a Duc d'Orleans, Louis Philippe by name, descended from a younger son of Louis XIII., married to a Sicilian Princess, and already beginning to abound in children; but the Orleans connection were barely tolerated at Court, and were secretly abhorred by the restored Bourbons. The King could not forget that the Duke's father, Egalité, had voted for the death of Louis XVI.; far less could the Duchess d'Angoulême forgive the man who was the son of one of her father's murderers; least of all did the Legitimists choose to ignore the fact that the Duc d'Orleans, when Duc de Chartres, had fought in the ranks of the Jacobin volunteers against the "Saviours of Society," that is to say, the Austrians and Prussians, summoned to the invasion of France by the proclamation of the Duke of Brunswick.

Old Louis Dixhuit, then, finding that his nephew, the Dauphin of the Future, was getting on but badly with Bonaparte's old generals, who would have none of his company, and that he was leading somewhat of a reckless life in Paris, discreetly married him, in the year '16, to Marie Caroline Ferdinande Louise de Bourbon, daughter of the Prince Royal of the Two Sicilies. This Marie Caroline was a delightfully pretty, vivacious, petulant, spoilt girl, who had been brought up to tell her beads, to eat sweetmeats, to play with a doll, and absolutely to do nothing else. She brought some of her *poupées* with her to Paris; and was wont to divert herself therewith in the intervals of Court receptions; until there came to her another doll to dandle, of real flesh and blood, and with eyes that moved without any string-pulling. In negotiating this alliance the crafty old king is said to have had in view the consolidation of the House of Bourbon upon the three thrones it then occupied in Italy, in Spain, and in France. The union of Charles Ferdinand and Marie Caroline promised at first to be a very happy one. Two daughters were born to them, but by the year 1819 one of these infants had died. Still, the Duke and Duchess were very young; and the chances of the detested Orleans connection ever dropping into the line of succession seemed too preposterous to think about. You see that it is not given to mankind to peruse the proof-sheets of the decrees of Fate. How one would "operate" on the Stock Exchange, if such a perusal were possible, to be sure!

There happened to be in Paris in 1820 a man named Louvel. It may be broadly said of him that he was cousin-german to Ravaillac, to Damiens, and to Jacques Clement; all of whom owned a common progenitor in the Devil. Louvel was a petty mechanic, and came from Versailles, where his father dealt in old clothes. Thirty-two years of age, a little weazened, wan, bilious man, with something the matter with his lungs—this Louvel, journeyman saddler or harness-maker, or something of that kind, I apprehend, had gotten some absurd nonsense into his head about Harmodius and Aristogeiton, with other pernicious rubbish instilled into his addled brain by a set of vagabonds—half fanatics, half scoundrels, and whole nuisances—who called themselves the Theophilanthropists, and professed to derive their Evangel from the sainted Jacobin Laréveillière and the immaculate *sans-culotte* Lepaux.

It occurred to Louvel—as it has occurred to many before and after that rascal—that the times were out of joint, and that he was born to set them right. The natural sequence to this, in his muddled mind, was that the Bourbons were wholly and solely responsible for the disjointed condition of things; and that if he could only contrive to cut the throat of a Bourbon Prince—say of the Duc de Berri—peace and prosperity would thenceforth reign; liberty, equality, and fraternity would flourish; and French Rentes, then stagnating at

56, would go up to par. How many regicides have bemused themselves with such Bedlamite day-dreams as these? The end of Louvel's reveries was that, with a dagger in his pocket, he began to lurk at night about the doors of theatres which he thought the Duc de Berri would visit. He followed him even to the churches; but, throughout the many months during which this frightful quest continued, he failed to grasp his prey. At length, on the 13th February, 1820, it being then High Carnival in Paris, it was announced that the Duc and Duchess de Berri would honour with their presence the Académie Royal de Musique, which was then situated in the Rue de Richelieu, over against the Bibliothèque Royale.

While they were enjoying the prospects

of the evening's entertainment—nay, while they were in the act of dressing for the opera ball, Louvel, his knife in his bosom, was watching at the Palace of the Elysée, in the Rue du Faubourg St. Honoré, where the Royal couple dwelt. Thence, about seven, he skulked away to the Opera House. It was Sunday—*le Dimanche Gras*—the first of the three "fat" days, which crown and close the Carnival. At eight o'clock Louvel was at the Royal entrance to the theatre: when the clattering of horses' hoofs, and the glare of the torches borne by the *dragons éclaireurs* announced the coming of the Duke and Duchess.

The distraught scoundrel rushed to the carriage door. This was his opportunity; yet curiously enough, he let it slip, confessing afterwards that the sight of the little Neapolitan Princess, young, smiling, and happy, had brought to his mind the recollection of a sister, to whom he was tenderly attached, and had, for a moment, imbued his black soul with something of the nature of pity.

Lady Macbeth (who was *not* mad, for a long time after being accessory to a murder), avowed, you will remember, the influence of a similar feeling when she gazed upon old King Duncan asleep. Yet the deed had got to be done, subsequently, for all the King's resemblance to the Thane of Cawdor's father-in-law. The compassionate compunction of the crazy journeyman-saddler did not endure for long. He prowled away into the Palais Royal, which was on the way to his lodging; but presently the Mad Devil was at him again. He slackened his pace, halted, turned back, and, to the Duke's destruction and his own, took up his post in front of the Opera House. Soon after eleven the carriages arrived to convey Royalty to its home. Louvel slipped after the vehicles, and entering the small deserted street called the Rue de Louvois, coolly stood at one of the horses' heads, as though he had belonged to the Court following. The Duke's servants said afterwards that they took the assassin for an agent of the police in plain clothes.* The shadow of the Opera House wall concealed his miserable countenance.

* This might well have been the case, as it is well known that Louis XVIII., mistrusting the fidelity of his Prefect of Police, maintained for his own private and particular use, and at his own expense, a corps of spies, who, in contradistinction to the orthodox *mouchards* of the Rue de Jerusalem, were known as "La Police du Château."

Meanwhile, the Duke and Duchess were in the theatre enjoying themselves. Another ducal couple were in the next box—their Highnesses of Orleans, indeed; and in the course of the evening Madame de Berri visited her Sicilian kinswoman, Madame d'Orleans. The Duc de Berri, on his part, embraced his cousin's children—notably the little Duc de Chartres, afterwards to be that Ferdinand d'Orleans who was killed in the Avenue de Neuilly, leaving a baby-boy who is now Comte de Paris, and the proximate "Dauphin." But the equerries knocked at the door, and warned Royalty that it was time to depart. The Duke, however, was in a jovial mood, and said that, when he had conducted his wife to her carriage, he would remain for awhile, and see the frolics of the Carnival to the top of the bent of their fooling. Downstairs the party came; bowing ushers, with lighted tapers, preceding them. The Duchess entered her carriage, handed in by her husband; while on the other side was her *gentilhomme d'honneur*, the Comte de Mesnard, and behind her the Comtesse de Béthisy, her lady-in-waiting. At this moment Louvel sprang like a tiger through the ranks of the soldiers of the Royal Guard, who were presenting arms; and seizing the left shoulder of the Duc de Berri with his left hand, stabbed him with all his might in the right side, leaving his dagger in the wound.

The rapidity of the act, the confusion of the bystanders, the uncertain light of the torches, prevented the Comte de Choiseul and M. de Mesnard, who were close to the assassin, from seizing him, and Louvel was enabled to dart away unpursued towards the Boulevard. He was captured, however, a very short time afterwards at the door of a café, where, almost incredible to relate, he had gone, as he said, "pour prendre des rafraichissements." And yet, looking closer into it, it is not improbable that the wretch may really have felt thirsty after such work. There is no need to tell in detail how the Demoniac, after being half torn to pieces by the populace — it is a pity they did not put him out of his mad misery then and there — was flung into the Conciergerie; kept almost entirely without sleep during the many weeks of the "instruction;" and at length tried before the Chamber of Peers, convicted, and guillotined in the white gaberdine and black veil of a parricide, on the Place de Grêve. He was luckier than his cousins-german, Ravaillac and the rest, who were racked and thumbscrewed, pinched and seared with redhot pincers, molten lead and resin, and similar *dolcezze*, and at last torn asunder by furious horses. At least "the ideas of 1789" saved Louvel from those judicial attentions.

Mortally wounded, Charles Ferdinand d'Artois, Duc de Berri, lingered for some hours in one of the antechambers of the Opera House. He was sensible, however, to the last, and, as has often been the case with princes in his condition, earnestly besought that no harm might be done to his murderer. His surviving daughter, just a year old, was brought to him. He stretched out his trembling arms to bless her, mur-

muring, "Poor child, may you be less unhappy than the rest of your family!" He little knew how many more misfortunes were in store for his fated race. His father, his brother Angoulême, his cousins of Orleans and of Bourbon-Conde, stood round his couch; and it was in the arms of his wife—no longer a petulant, vivacious, spoilt child, but a woman destined to be a Heroine—that he died. "Caroline," he whispered, "take care of yourself, for the sake of the child that you bear."

This was the first revelation of the birth of an heir to his name. A little before the Duke's death the poor old King arrived. Extreme unction had been administered by the Bishop of Chartres; and then the Curtain fell, and the most tragic of all the dramas that had ever been played within the walls of that garish theatre came to an end.

Seven months and sixteen days after the murder of Charles Ferdinand, Duc de Berri, at the Opera House—which, shortly after his death, was demolished to its last stone, with a view to the erection of an expiatory chapel on its site; (the Place Louvois is yet bare, and the Third Restoration may yet build the chapel of expiation)—the widowed Marie Caroline gave birth, at the Palace of the Tuileries, to a man child. This was Henri Charles Ferdinand Dieudonné de France, born on the 29th of September, 1820. It is as well to be particular concerning the date of his birth, as it is one which, in combination with that of his father's death, those evilly disposed to the Elder Branch never failed malevolently to recite. The pious Legitimists, on their part, were more pleased to remember that the "Heaven-sent" Prince first saw the light on St. Michael's Day. That Archangel was famous for stamping out the lives of infernal dragons—Rafaelle and Correggio have shown us how;—and all good French Catholics saw, in 1820, in the birth of the young Prince on the feast of St. Michael, a special sign of protection from Heaven against the dreadful plots of the Revolutionists.

Revolutionary conspiracies were annoyingly prevalent in 1820. There had been, also, some very ill-natured rumours current just before the little Prince's appearance—rumours of which we need say no more than that they were as spiteful as those which obtained among Whig gossips just before our Glorious Revolution, when Mary of Modena gave birth, at St. James's, to a little Prince of Wales, afterwards to be known as the Old Pretender. To confound the calumniators, it was determined, in the case of the Duchesse de Berri, that to her *accouchement* should be given " an authentic publicity, in conformity with the ancient usages of the Monarchy;" and Marshal Suchet, " with several officers of the guard of the Tuileries, were present at the birth, as irrefragable witnesses of the maternity of the Duchess." Royalty, you see, has its responsibilities as well as its rights. At least we of the middle classes are entitled to be born without the *surveillance* of an officer of the Grenadier Guards and an Inspector of Police.

Now that spiteful gossip is dead and buried, one may fitly recall, in respect to Henri de France, that which Sir Godfrey Kneller used to say about the Chevalier de St. George. "Dey say dey bring him in a warming-pan," the irate German was wont to exclaim. "*Ach, Himmel!* I bainted his fader and his moder fifty time over. Look at his face, and tell me dat he is not his fader and his moder's son, if you dare." A glance at the portrait of the Comte de Chambord should be sufficient to confute all sceptics. He is, in the first instance, wonderfully like his uncle, Louis XVIII., when, young, and known as "Monsieur," Comte de Provence. In the next place he has his father's eyes, his mother's mouth and chin,* the exact "Bour-

* As well as I can judge, allowing for the moustache and beard, and, comparing the face with a charming

bon" lip, and the "Bourbon" mien, port, and expression in every lineament of his countenance. The old King was one of the first personages who beheld his grand-nephew. He took the child in his arms; and, in obedience to a quaint tradition current in his house, moistened the lips of the newborn infant with some drops of wine. The ceremonial—an old Gaulish one, perhaps—of "wine before milk" had been observed, it was said, at the birth of Henri Quatre.

Nevertheless, the ill-natured tongues could not be kept quiet. A mysterious document, protesting against the legitimacy of the birth, found its way into some of the Lon-

portrait of the Duchess, engraved in our "Monthly Magazine" for 1820, the Comte de Chambord must have been, twenty years ago, ere the atrocious beard-movement made Englishmen self-satisfied, slovenly, and "smouchy, wonderfully like his mother.

don newspapers. It is curious to think that it might have been read by a certain Prometheus raging just then on his rock at St. Helena—the sharpest of the vulture's talons which were tearing him being, perchance, the thoughts of his own little boy, mewed up yonder at Schönbrünn, under the guardianship of wearisome Austrian chamberlains. The protest was attributed to the Duke of Orleans, who promptly disavowed it; but Louis Philippe frankly admitted that he had not placed faith in the authenticity of the Event until it had been attested by the word of honour of Marshal Suchet. "Je l'ai vu de mes propres yeux," were the explicit words of Monsieur le Maréchal: and the legionaries who had carried Cæsar's eagles were not given to telling lies.

As for France in general, sympathy soon

grew into enthusiasm, and rejoicings at the auspicious occurrence were universal. Monsieur le Vicomte de Chateaubriand hastened to salute the little Prince as "L'Enfant du Miracle;" which, albeit the epithet was very pretty and poetical, was somewhat of an Irish kind of compliment, and had better have been left unsaid. As a rule, the advocates of hereditary monarchy would prefer that heirs presumptive did *not* come into the world miraculously. The foreign Ambassadors accredited to the Court of the Tuileries—those of their number, at least, who were of the Holy Alliance way of thinking—hailed the Royal baby as "the Child of Europe;" and it is edifying to mark, under similar circumstances, the perverse addictedness of diplomatic and other official personages towards circumlocution and hyperbole. Everybody, surely, should have been satisfied with honest Marshal Suchet's voucher, in addition to the knowledge of the fact that Henri Dieudonné was the son of his father, Charles Ferdinand, Duc de Berri.

II.

THE EXILE OF FORTY YEARS.

INNUMERABLE appointments and promotions in the Legion of Honour, the revived order of the Saint Esprit, and the newly-created guild of St. Michael took place in honour of the birth of Henri de France. Royal munificence, amnesties, favours of every kind were showered down on the people. The young mother had only to ask, and her every request was granted by the delighted old King. The child's cradle—a miracle in itself of rare woods, ivory, quilted satin, and mother-o'-pearl—was the most sumptuous ever seen in France since—well, since when? Since that day, perchance, when, with Kings and

Kaisers for sponsors, and with consecrated water from the River Jordan in the sculptured font, an Archbishop of Paris baptised the son of Napoleon the Great.

As a mark of Royal gratitude and high condescension towards the noble City of the Garonne—the City, which had, in 1814, evinced her loyalty to the House of Bourbon (not without some encouragement and assistance from a certain Arthur Wellesley, Duke of Wellington) by welcoming within her walls Monseigneur le Duc d'Angoulême, and had again earned distinction in 1815 by protesting against the return from Elba of the Corsican Usurper, while offering an asylum to Madame la Duchesse d'Angoulême—the infant Henri was created Duc de Bordeaux. Just fifty years afterwards, in that same City of the Garonne, the legislative compromise known as the "Pacte de Bordeaux" was concluded.

As for his comital title, that designation he derived from the castle and estate of Chambord, an ancient Royal demesne near Blois. It had become national property; and, being for sale in 1820, was in danger of falling into the hands of a gang of speculators called "La Bande Noire," who were in the habit of purchasing historic mansions for the Vandalic purpose of pulling them down, selling the land in small lots to farmers, and disposing of the valuable *débris* of the antique castles, such as sculptures, carvings, painted windows, ceilings, and oak panelling, to the bric-à-brac dealers. A public subscription rescued the Château de Chambord from the Iconoclasts of the Black Band; and the mansion and estate were presented, as a testimonial of the affection of the French people, to the baby Duke. When he came to man's estate, in the tenth year of his dreary exile, he assumed the *quasi-incognito* title of Comte de Chambord, just as Peter the Great in his travels was called "Comte du Nord;" Louis XVIII., in exile, Comte de Lille;" the Duchesse d'Angoulême, "Comtesse de Marnes;" and the ex-King Joseph Bonaparte, "Comte de Survilliers." The estate of Chambord was not confiscated when Louis Philippe, by the cleverest of "flukes," ascended the throne; nor was the exiled Prince forced to sell the testimonial of French affection; and throughout the duration of the July Monarchy, together with that of the Second Empire, the Château de Chambord remained untenanted but intact, under the care of a few ancient servitors, clad in the Bourbon livery.

The first ten years of the little Duke's life were passed as those of heirs presumptive to great thrones generally have been passed. He was, of course, lapped in luxury, swaddled in obsequious homage, and weaned on adulation. His great-uncle, King Louis, died; his grandfather, King Charles X., ascended the throne—and notwithstanding his splendid coronation and consecration in the Cathedral of Rheims—did somewhat badly as a Monarch; so badly, indeed, that by the end of July, 1830, the mob were in the Tuileries, the army was disorganised, the crown in the kennel, and the Monarchy nowhere.

In the midst of the last spasms of

expiring Royalty a knot of fanatical Legitimists hastened to the palace of St. Cloud, where the Duchess de Berri was residing with the young Prince, for the purpose of persuading her to waylay the Duke of Orleans—soon to be appointed Lieutenant-General of the kingdom—on his way from Neuilly; to extort from him a promise of fidelity; or, if necessary, to have him seized by force and detained as a hostage. Then the Duchesse was to enter Paris, and traverse the boulevards with her son in her arms, imploring the compassion of the people for " the child of a martyr, and the victim of an old man's imbecility."

The brave young Duchess highly approved of this plan; a number of plucky Legitimist gentlemen were ready to aid

her with their swords; and there is
no saying but that the madcap enterprise
might have succeeded had it not been for
the veto of the impracticable Charles X.,
conveyed through the Baron de Damas.
The unhappy King was utterly discouraged, and had lost all hope of regaining
the crown, sacrificed by his consummate
obstinacy and folly. It may be said almost
literally that the Bourbon Monarchy in
July, 1830, tumbled over like a house of
cards; for when all was lost, and the
raging mob were on their way to St. Cloud,
Charles X. quietly sat down to a game
of whist with the Duchesse de Berri, the
Duc de Luxembourg, and the Duc de
Duras. Monsieur de Mortemart came to
tell him that the troops were mutinying,
but that there was some chance of their

returning to their allegiance if the Duc d'Angoulême were permitted to place himself at their head. "Wait till to-morrow," announced Charles Dix, scoring, it may be presumed, his "honours." Then his Majesty went to bed; and on the morrow the Medes and Persians were at the gate, and his kingdom was given to another.

Flying from St. Cloud to the Trianon, and thence to Rambouillet, a wretched reunion took place of these bankrupt Bourbons. The grey discrowned King, the enraged Duchesse de Berri, the bewildered little Duc de Bordeaux, and she—the heiress of unending woe—the disconsolate Duchesse d'Angoulême, all met together. *C'était un joli ménage.* From Rambouillet Charles X. wrote a solemn letter of mingled entreaty and command to the Duc d'Orleans, formally abdicating the crown in favour of his grandson Henri. The Dauphin, he continued, alluding to the Duc d'Angoulême, had likewise resigned his rights in favour of his nephew. Upon this the infatuated Charles proceeded to order Louis Philippe, on his allegiance as Lieutenant-General of the Kingdom—he was already *de facto* King of France—to proclaim the accession to the throne of Henry Cinq; to take all the necessary measures pertaining to his office in order to settle the form of government during the new Sovereign's minority; and to communicate the gracious intentions of himself, Charles X., to the diplomatic body. And so his Late Majesty concluded, " I renew to you, my cousin, the assurance of the sentiments with which I am your affectionate cousin, CHARLES." An archdeacon could not have more gracefully fulfilled archidiaconal functions.

The poor old gentleman shortly afterwards faded away from Rambouillet to Maintenon, a château belonging to the Noailles family. This was on the 4th of August, 1830. On the 5th the Royal family took their departure for the coast: the Duchesse de Berri leading her son by the hand. The Royal widow had by this time recovered something of her old petulance and vivacity; for contemporary chronicles tell us that when she left the Château of Maintenon she was dressed *in male attire;* and as she lifted her son into the travelling-carriage she exclaimed cheerfully,—"Il ne faut plus songer au départ, mais au retour"—"Never mind the going away; let's think of coming back." Everybody can come back, so it would appear—save the dead.

The exiles were so poor that, when they arrived at Dreux, they were forced to sell some of the plate they had with them to defray their travelling expenses. Reaching Cherbourg, after a long and dolorous journey, the luckless group embarked on board a vessel which had been provided for their conveyance to England. A few officers and a handful of privates of his extinguished Garde Royale accompanied the King to the place of embarkation. They handed him the regimental flags. "I receive your standards," he replied, in a voice choked with sobs, "but this child shall one day return them to you," and he touched with a trembling hand the forehead of the Duc de Bordeaux. It was a parody—a respectable and affecting one, but still a parody—of the adieux of Napoleon to his Old Guard in the courtyard at Fontainebleau.

With that dismal scene on the quay at Cherbourg commenced the Forty Years' Exile of Henri de France. Forty years! The Story of his Life, so far as his public acts and deeds during that period are concerned, might be epitomed in forty lines of print; yet what an immensity of sorrow must not the banished Prince have endured in that wide span of two score summers! It is only recently that the veil which for so long a time has screened the individuality of the Comte de Chambord from public view has been even partially lifted; but day by day the sum of facts will increase and accumulate, and the world will be put into full possession of all the circumstances connected with the career of the last "Son of St. Louis."

The ascertained points in his history since August, 1830, may be very briefly stated. From Cherbourg the Royal Family of France crossed the Channel to Weymouth, whence they proceeded to Lulworth Castle, in Dorsetshire. Their next resting-place was at the Royal Palace of Holyrood, at Edinburgh; but at the end of 1832, Charles X. and his meagre train of kindred and dependents again became wanderers, and took up their quarters in the Castle of the Hradschin, at Prague: the rambling old Bohemian *schloss* now inhabited by the abdicated Austrian Kaiser, Ferdinand. For three years and seven months did they abide in the Hradschin; after that they established themselves at

Goritz, in Illyria, where Chárles X. died, on the 6th of November, 1836. The Duc de Bordeaux, after his grandfather's death, continued to reside at Goritz with his uncle, Louis Antoine de France—whom bigoted Legitimists persisted, notwithstanding the renunciation of Rambouillet, in styling "Louis XIX."—with his aunt, Marie Thérèse, and his sister Louise. On the 28th July, 1841, the young Prince, who had been passing some time at the Castle of Kirchberg, near Vienna, nearly lost his life by a fall from his horse. He escaped with a broken hip-bone. It may here be stated that his early education had been conducted mainly by the Comte de Barante, the Duc de Levis, and General de Latour-Foissac. Accompanied by his preceptors, he travelled in succession through England,

Germany, and Italy, settling for some months in Rome, where he devoted himself, it is stated, very sedulously to artistic study.

He abode, in the Eternal City, at the Palazzo Conti. At the Palazzo Madama, not far from him, there was then dwelling another Exile—an old, a very old lady, whose maiden name was Letizia Ranolini, but who is better known as "Madame Mère"—the mother of Napoleon. It would be strange to enquire whether the grandmamma of the little King of Rome ever crossed carriages with the grandson of Charles X. on the Pincian Hill. The sojourn of the Duc de Bordeaux in Rome, was eminently distasteful to the French Government; and the Ambassador of France at the Vatican, M. Chabaud-Latour, went so far as to hold threatening language to Pope Gregory XVI., hinting at the possibility of a French squadron appearing off Civita Vecchia if the Holy Father persisted in receiving the exiled Bourbon.

In 1843 the Duc de Bordeaux came to England—to London, where a residence in Belgrave-square had been prepared for him—and his modest mansion soon became the shrine of a numerous and influential pilgrimage of Legitimists from France. Conspicuously among these devotees of the Right Divine were the Baron de Larcy, and four other members of the Chamber of Deputies— MM. de Valmy, Berryer, Chateaubriand, and the Duc de FitzJames. The visit of these gentlemen to Belgrave-square was regarded by the French Ministry in the light of a political and anti-Orleanist demonstration. M. Guizot, then at the head of Louis Philippe's Cabinet, was furious, and, on their return to France, the five Legitimist Deputies had no option save to resign their seats in the Chamber. Their constituents forthwith re-elected them; and the "incident" terminated, fortunately, without anybody being sent to prison. M. de Larcy, it may be mentioned, is the same gentleman who not long since accepted, under the Republican presidency of M. Thiers, the portfolio of Minister of Commerce.

In 1845 died the uncle of Henri de France, the Duc d'Angoulême. Shortly after this event, the Prince—to be Duc de Bordeaux no longer—warned the Great Powers that, as Head of the House of Bourbon, he protested against the dynastic changes which had taken place since 1830 in France, and against the usurpation of the crown on the part of Louis Philippe d'Orleans. He very gravely and amply formulated his own inalienable rights to the throne; but added that he was unwilling to insist upon the vindication of his claims until, according to his conscience and conviction, the moment had arrived when his presence in his native country was imperatively demanded and might become veritably useful. Thus, he signified his intention to assume for the present, in his relations with foreign Courts, the title of Comte de Chambord.

Having launched this manifesto—of which neither Europe in general nor France in particular took the slightest notice—the Comte de Chambord, his aunt, and his sister removed from Goritz to the Castle of Frohsdorf, an estate heretofore belonging to the ancient French family of De Blacas. In 1845 the Comte married, at Gratz, in Styria, the Archduchess Marie Thérèse of Austria and Este, Princess-Ducal of Modena. No offspring has been the fruit of this union. The Comte's sister, " Mademoiselle " Louise de France, became the Consort of the Infante of Spain, and Hereditary Prince and Duke of Parma and Piacenza, a Sovereign of tendencies somewhat too mediæval—he was an atrocious miscreant—and who was very mediævally and completely assassinated one Sunday morning in Parma by a countryman, to a member of whose family he had done a foul wrong. His widow governed the Duchy as Regent during the minority of her son, Duke Robert, until the Duchies of Parma and Piacenza were swallowed up by the "Sub-Alpine King" Victor Emmanuel of Sardinia. Let it be likewise borne in mind, as another of the odd points of contact between the Bourbons and the Buonapartes, that these Duchies of Parma and Piacenza, with the principality of Guastalla, formed the appanage allotted by the Congress of Vienna to Maria Louisa, ex-Empress of the French, and Archduchess of Austria, when Napoleon was sent to Elba. As for the spouse of the Comte de Chambord, her father, the Duke of Modena, was another of the petty Italian potentates dispossessed in 1859-60 by the omnivorous "Rè Sabaudo." The confidential friends of the Comte, the Duke of Levis in particular, have frequently been blamed for having favoured the marriage of Henri de France with the Modenese Princess, who is two years older than her lord.

The personal appearance of the Comte de Chambord is comely, dignified, and agreeable. As we have before hinted, his profile resembles that of his grand-uncle, Louis XVIII.—the moustache and whiskers, of a slightly Austrian-cavalry-cut, being allowed for. His demeanour is easy, graceful, and unstudied. He is slightly above the middle height, and more than slightly given to *embonpoint*, the family failing—if it be not the family favour—of the Elder Branch. His forehead is remarkably high and smooth. His voice is sonorous and peculiarly attractive. His acquirements as a linguist—especially in English—are, it is reported,

remarkable; he is in every respect accom
plished, and is a very brilliant conversa
tionalist. The Prince is an early riser
seldom quitting his apartment later than six
in the morning. The day commences with
the examination and co-ordination of an ex
ceedingly voluminous correspondence, to
which he gives his personal attention
answering a large number of letters with
his own hand. The remainder of the epis
tolary duties fall to the share of M. de
Blacas. Next the French and other news
papers, of which weighty packets are every
day received at Frohsdorf, are glanced
through and sorted; the Prince again per
sonally superintending their perusal, making
numerous extracts and clippings with his
own Royal scissors, and filing the journals
for future reference with extraordinary pa

tience and exactitude. Nor is this painstaking methodism, perhaps, to be marvelled at. Napoleon, at St. Helena, used to sort his snuff-boxes, and divide his cameos into categories. The time must have hung so heavily on our hands these forty years past!

From journalism the Prince proceeds to equitation. He is passionately fond of horsemanship — his broken hip-bone notwithstanding—and his stables are magnificently stocked. Towards nine in the morning he starts for an airing on horseback, accompanied by a single servant, or by some gentlemen on a visit to Frohsdorf. At half-past ten he returns to breakfast—a very simple meal, the Prince being neither "gourmand" nor "gourmet." The repast never lasts longer than half an hour; the

Comte taking the head of the table; Madame la Comtesse, sitting on his right; and the *vis-à-vis* being occupied by one of his confidential friends. The seat to the left is reserved for any visitor who may be staying at the Château. The meal over, the Prince adjourns to the smoking-room, there to sip a cup of coffee. He talks freely upon ordinary topics, receives visitors, and gives audience to persons coming on business. During the remainder of the day he usually devotes two or three hours to writing; after which, accompanied by the Princess, he takes a ride in the park, or in the environs of Frohsdorf: returning to dinner, which is served at seven o'clock, and lasts precisely one hour. Beyond the ordinary rules of exalted etiquette, which are, of course, rigidly observed, there is no restraint on the conversation that concludes the evening; and by ten o'clock all is quiet in the Castle of Frohsdorf. What a life! The days pass, and *do* resemble each other and so they have passed, with but very few intervals of change, for much more than a quarter of a century. Let it be also mentioned that the Comte and Comtesse are both passing wealthy; but that a large portion of their revenues is annually expended in pensions, annuities and donations to the neighbouring poor, and to indigent French people of all ranks and classes in society. Such, as I have been enabled to sketch his story and that of his belongings, is the Man Henri Dieudonné de France, of whom his heroic mother, the Duchesse de Berri, wrote twenty year since to an old and faithful adherent—" If he were known, *as he is*, I have not the slightest doubt that his name would become at once and universally popular—as popular as that of Henri Quatre, even with those who are now most prejudiced against him. It is what all who see him feel, and you will not wonder at his mother acknowledging, and being proud of it."

III.

ADVENTURES OF THE DUCHESSE DE BERRI.

FIFTEEN years ago there was a Silent City by the Sea—a city in whose broad and narrow streets the tide rose every day, now green in hue, according to Holland; now blue, according to Stanfield; now grey, according to Canaletto; now all the colours of the rainbow, according to Turner. I speak of the City in the past tense; for, albeit there is still a matchless Queen of the Adriatic—although the twin giants still keep watch over the staircase whence Marino Faliero cursed "the Gehenna of the waters," and her serpent-seed—although the Campanile yet proudly dominates the cupolas of

St. Mark, and the Rialto yet spans the Canalazzo—the Venice of the present has become, so lovers of the picturesque assert, somewhat of a vulgar place. The P. and O. steamers puff and snort opposite Danieli's; and unromantic tugs and coal lighters make turbid the waters of Malamocco. Vulgar little boys cry cheap newspapers and cigar-lights at the doors of Florian's and the Specchi; shipbrokers and stevedores wrangle on the Piazzetta, and have driven away the ancient turbaned Turk, who was wont to sit, grand, cross-legged, and imperturbable, at the Caffè dell' Aurora; and Cook's tourists pervade the Ducal Palace, cry for bitter ale at the Albergo Vittoria, and compare the Bridge of Sighs with Temple Bar.

But fifteen years since Venice was

the silentest of silent seaports. Songless rowed her gondoliers — those *barcaruoli* who used to chant strophes from Tasso, but are now, under the influence of Constitutional liberty, given to whistling Garibaldi's hymn, or the Gendarmes' song from "Geneviève de Brabant." So silent was St. Mark's Place that an assemblage of more than three persons on the Broglio was considered a crowd, to be regarded with suspicion by the police; while the shipping of the port rarely exceeded a few *goelette* from Pola, and *speronari* from Chioggia, with perhaps a stray collier from Cardiff, the skipper of which might be met with, in a tall hat, with the ship's papers in a tin box under his arm, drifting in a gondola towards the British Consulate—occasionally apostrophising the boatman as a "left-handed lubber"—and wearing, altogether very much the aspect of a fly in amber. There was a magnificent Opera-house in this silent city; but it had been shut up for years. There was a sumptuous Royal Palace; but its walls were as desolate as those of Balclutha; save once in a way, when an Austrian Archduke dropped in from Trieste to pass a division of Croat Grenadiers in review on the Campo di Marzo; to grumble because the structural arrangements of Venice did not render possible the evolutions of cavalry in the Ramo de' Fuseri—there was one animal, reputed to be a horse, at the Giardini Pubblici, where they let him out, at ten kreutzers for a quarter of an hour's ride: but subsequent inquiries have rather tended to the conclusion that he was a zebra tha had strayed from a menagerie—

and to hold a levee which was mainly attended by officers of the Austrian garrison, Austrian Government clerks, and Austrian police spies.

There were many proud old Venetian families in the place, but they shut themselves up in their damp old palaces, living on *polenta* and *fritture*, and railing, in undertones, against the *Tedeschi*. There were many noble and beautiful ladies in the city, but they very rarely came abroad:—when they did, they shrouded themselves in mourning garments, and, closely veiled, sat far back on the black cushions in the black state-rooms of their gondolas. There was no trade, no commerce to speak of, and only one newspaper—a poverty-stricken Official Gazette—" printed on grey paper with blunt type," in which his

Imperial, Royal, and Apostolic Majesty Francis Joseph, Kaiser of Austria, King of Hungary and Bohemia, was generally spoken of as being only a little lower than the angels; while Victor Emmanuel was likened, at least twice a week, to Barabbas, to Maximilian Robespierre, and to Herod of Jewry. This was the city in which Herr Zimmermann might have written his celebrated tractate on Solitude; or St. Jerome might have found, in the Lion of St. Mark, silent and disconsolate on the summit of his pillar, a substitute for his four-footed friends of the desert. Nevertheless, the Silent City stood, imperishable, in the sea; and on its every stone were, to English minds, indelibly inscribed the names of Samuel Rogers, John Ruskin, and George Gordon, Lord Byron. But for their writings, Venice might have faded altogether out of modern memory, as Antioch and Trebizond, as Samarcand and Ispahan have faded.

Silence, Mr. Carlyle says, is golden; still the least silent season in Venice, fifteen years since, was the golden afternoon. Then a little life would ruffle the bosom of the sleepy waters. Then, sometimes, the stray sojourner, in this abode of Melancholy, might espy a sable shallop waiting at the marble steps of a certain palace on the Grand Canal—a quaint old mansion in the Byzantine Gothic style of the fifteenth century, with quadrilobed *œils de bœuf* over the arcades of the casements, and a great ogival-headed portal. Antiquaries knew this house very well as the Palazzo Cavalli. It was, moreover, dear to Italian patriots as having been the residence of Alessandro Pepoli, a famous Venetian author; but if the stray sojourner asked his boatman what was the designation of the house, he would be told that it was the Palazzo Chambord.

Presently, watching the barque waiting at the steps, he would descry that, mingled with the usual hearselike decorations of the tilted cabin—the ebon carvings, the tufted housings of black velvet, the fringes and tassels of sable silk—there were sundry little gold scutcheons charged with the lilies of France, surmounted by a crown-regal, and interspersed with the initials "M.C.," woven into a monogram. Further pursuing his inquiries, he might have learnt that "il Conte di Chambord, Rè di Francia, grand' amico de' Tedeschi," frequently came to Venice to visit his mother, "la

Signora Duchessa di Berri," and that the waiting gondola was hers. By-and-by, a trim, alert, little old lady, with very white ringlets, very bright blue eyes, and a blooming peach-like complexion:—clad in deep mourning, and wearing a black lace mantilla, after the manner of the Milanese ladies, but forbearing to draw the drapery over her face, as was then the sulky Venetian mode, would come tripping down the steps of the Palazzo Chambord, attended by a single lady in mourning, to enter her gondola. Her draperies would be duly arranged on the low cushions; a milky-white little Bolognese poodle, with a crimson cord and tassel round his neck, would be installed by her side; the little old lady would give one sharp, skilful rattle on the gamut of her fan as a signal; and away would go her shallop, the oars softly plashing in the still waters of the 'prisoned Adriatic.

No one could mistake the Duchesse de Berri's marine equipage; since her gondoliers, instead of being dressed in the open-breasted vests, the wide, striped trousers, the crimson sashes and Phrygian caps so dear to the "Hansom cabmen of the sea," were attired in straight-cut blue coats, tall hats with gold-laced bands and cockades of white sarcenet, crimson plush smalls, and brown gaiters. They wore shoulder-knots, their hair was powdered—these very queer toilers of the sea. Imagine John Thomas at the helm, and Jeames of Berkeley-square at the prow, and—*risum teneatis?* The pretty little old Duchess rather liked being looked at than otherwise: she kept her state-room door open, and sat well forward on her ottoman. The white flannel-clad Austrian officers, the foreign consuls, the few—the very few *Austriacante* members of the Venetian aristocracy who passed her, gravely saluted the illustrious little woman. The common people of Venice rather admired her. She would land at the Molo; potter about the drapery stores of the Merceria and the jewellers' shops of the Procuratie Vecchie; never failed to set her watch by the antique dial in the Torre dell' Orologio; and was always followed back to her bark by a mob of sympathising beggars, to whom she was a sublunary providence. She was the most charitable of womankind, and would have given her little head away had it been loose.

There ran a rumour that she and her

lady-in-waiting had once sat a whole half-hour under the arcades outside Florian's, reading the Legitimist *Gazette de France*, while John Thomas or Jeames of Berkeley-square—gondoliers afloat, running footmen on shore—brought ices and macaroons from the *caffè*. It was whispered that, in the recesses of her stately old palace, she yet sang, to the guitar she played so deftly, the sweet old canzonets of her beloved Naples, and that she was a wonderful hand at piquet. "Almeno," the Venetians used to say, "è Italiana." At least, she was not a *Tedesca*. Let us hope that, when her time came, Betty gave her cheek a touch more red, to make her comfortable, and that her end was Peace.

Now let the Silent City in the Sea and the pretty old French dame in her gondola be entirely erased from memory; and let us go back to the year 1830, and to Marie Caroline de Bourbon, the widowed Duchess de Berri, the mother of a young Pretender —herself youthful, high-spirited, giddy, enterprising, brave as the Cid, obstinate enough for several ladies, and, like the Mrs. Bond of the nursery legend, in the matter of the ducks which declined to come and be killed, "in a very great rage." She was destined to pass through a series of adventures fully as perilous and even more romantic than those which fell to the lot of Charles II. after Worcester, and of Charles Edward after Culloden; for a parallel to which we must go back to the life of Benvenuto Cellini, or to Swift's Memoirs of Captain Crichton.

Poor old Charles Dix had retired, utterly

disorganised and "played out," to Holyrood; but the valiant little Duchess was of the precise opinion expressed by a Celebrated Character immortalised by Milton, that "all was not lost." Stung to resistance by high disdain and a sense of injured merit, her thoughts turned at once to the traditional home of devotion to her race—La Vendée. There the deeds of Stofflet, Charette, and La Roche Jacquelin might be repeated; there the Breton warcry, "Eparpillez-vous, mes gars!" might once more be heard in the Bocage, as the Chouans, deriding volleys of musketry, scattered themselves behind bushes, and picked off the detested "Bleus" from their covert. It was on the 29th of May, 1832, that, having formed the resolution of setting France in a blaze in the cause of Henri Cinq, the Duchess arrived, in the *Carlo Alberto* steamer, off Marseilles.

Some wild notions had been entertained by the Legitimists of the feasibility of an insurrectionary movement in the Provençal city itself. It was a very stormy night, and the captain of the *Carlo Alberto* proposed standing out in the offing until morning; but the Duchess insisted on a boat being lowered, declaring that she would reach the shore alone. "It was a peculiarity in Her Royal Highness's character," wrote General Dermoncourt of her, "to adhere more strongly to her resolutions when any opposition was offered to them." So the boat was lowered; and the Duchess, accompanied only by MM. de Ménars and de Bourmont, was rowed to land. Having reached a desolate spot on the coast, Marie Caroline wrapped herself up in a cloak, and quietly went to sleep: the two faithful gentlemen keeping guard over her. Meanwhile, the knot of Legitimist conspirators in Marseilles, with whom the Duchess had been in correspondence, had drawn up the curtain for the performance of their preposterous drama. It proved the shortest of farces. They succeeded in hauling down the Tricolor from the steeple of St. Laurent's Church, in hoisting the White Flag in its place, and in sounding the alarm-bell of the old fane to serve as a tocsin. But the drums of the garrison beat to arms, and the constituted authorities very soon succeeded in replacing the tricoloured banner on St. Laurent's spire. This intelligence, brought by faithful emissaries to the

Duchess, reached her on the morrow of her landing; but it was with the greatest difficulty that she could be dissuaded from tempting fortune in Marseilles. At last she consented to take refuge in a charcoal-burner's hut, while Bourmont went to make inquiries.

He very soon returned with tidings that the insurrection had been crushed as easily as though it had been a decayed apple under the wheel of a barrow, and that the gendarmerie, having an inkling of the Duchess's landing, were in hot pursuit of her. As for the *Carlo Alberto*, a French Government frigate had, by the simple process of opening her ports and running out the guns on her near side, prevailed on the Sardinian steamer to give the Provençal coast a wide berth.

Two alternatives now remained to Marie Caroline—either to escape by some unfrequented Alpine pass into Piedmont, or to turn westward, cross the greatest breadth of France, and seek an asylum in La Vendée. Her determination was akin to that recently expressed, under somewhat different circumstances, by the King of Italy, when the Papal party suggested that he should leave Rome—"Here we are; and here we will remain." The Duchess declared that, having re-entered France, she intended to stop there; and that her resolve was forthwith to bend her footsteps towards Britanny.

There was neither horse nor mule, nor carriage available for the journey; but the mother of the Duc de Bordeaux having declared that she was a very good

alker, and the charcoal-burner having
fered his services as a guide, the little party,
ielded by the shades of night, left the
ashore. At the other extremity of the
y they could distinguish the Phocæan
ty, and its numerous lights, twinkling like
ars. "Adieu, Marseille!" cried the
eery Duchess; "on retournera t'em-
asser, la belle." So out they went into
e night. It was so dark that they could
ith difficulty see their way before them;
t for five consecutive hours did they plod
d stumble onwards. At last the charcoal-
rner guide came to a full stop, confessing
at he had lost his way; and at the same
me the Duchess was fain to avow that she
as worn out, and could walk no farther.
gain she wrapped herself up in a cloak,
d, with a portmanteau for a pillow, went

G

to sleep as soundly as though she had been reposing on eider-down, beneath the *lambris dorés* of the Pavilion Marsan.

The faithful gentlemen—surely they must have been of the same stock with those valient Gardes du Corps who fell sword in hand on the staircase at Versailles, hurling back to the last the hideous Mœnads who were howling for the blood of Marie Antoinette—once more kept watch over "La Belle Bourbonnaise." She awoke at dawn; and, perceiving a country-house close by, inquired of a peasant to whom it belonged. She was told that the villa was the property of a furious Republican, who was, in addition, mayor of the adjacent commune. "Very well," quoth Marie Caroline; "conduct me thither." Turning to her amazed dependents, she told them that they must now part. M. de Bourmont was commanded forthwith to repair to Nantes, there to await her coming; M. de Ménars was instructed to proceed to Montpelier, not to stir thence until he received further orders. "Adieu, gentlemen," concluded the little Tragedy Queen; "I wish you a safe journey, and may God be with you." She gave them her hand to kiss, and the trio parted.

The remainder of *her* Story belongs much more to the domain of romance than to that of sober history. The undaunted Marie Caroline walked coolly into the *salle à manger* of the Mayor, and, accosting that functionary, said, "Sir, you are a Republican, and a Government officer; and I, a proscribed fugitive, have come to ask an asylum at your hands. I am the Duchesse de Berri."

What could the Republican Mayor, being mortal, and a Frenchman besides, with a pretty woman in distress confronting him—beshrew the mayor who would make out such a suppliant's *mittimus!*—do, save tell the Duchess that his house was at her service. Upon this Marie Caroline, still cool as a cucumber, went on to explain that she required, not only refreshment and a bed, but a passport to enable her to proceed to Montpelier. And in Montpelier, on the following evening, the undismayed Duchess accordingly found herself. There Marie Caroline rejoined M. de Ménars, with whom and another devoted adherent she travelled with fictitious passports to La Vendée.

Arrived in Brittany, she determined, in spite of the remonstrances of all her friends, to send out the Fiery Cross into the

Bocage. M. Berryer posted down from Paris to implore her to relinquish her rash enterprise, but in vain. The Vendean leaders themselves entreated her to pause; but the obstinate little lady challenged them on their allegiance: "Are you for God and the King, or are you not? If you are, *en avant!* if you are not, *sortez!*"

When Beauty (with the Right Divine to back it) commands, what can Duty (egged on by Gallantry) do but obey? When Juno adjured Æolus in the Cave of the Winds to hurl destruction on the Trojan fleet, she was fain to offer him the hand of Deiopeia as a "material consideration." The Breton Loyalists needed no such bribe to tempt them once more to vindicate the device: "Ung Roy, ung Foy, ung Loy."

Forty-five Chouan gentlemen, many of

them nobles, with two peasants who ha[d]
learned to play the light infantry bugle, me[t]
at the Chateau of La Pénissière de l[a]
Cour, there to raise the standard of rebel
lion. In this house they were beleaguere[d]
by a detachment of the 29th Regiment
They barricaded themselves, and a terribl[e]
fusillade commenced. Then the Orleanis[t]
soldiery set fire to the chateau; and in th[e]
conflagration of this obscure, but gloriou[s]
Hougoumont nearly all the Chouan gentle
men perished. They died, crying "Viv[e]
Henri Cinq!" One of the peasant bugl[e]
players succumbed early in the siege
the other, *with three bullets in his body*
continued to sound his puny trump until h[e]
fell fainting into the burning ruins. Hav[e]
such deeds never been equalled, neve[r]
surpassed? Think of the Jacobite gentle

men after the '45, drawn on their hurdles, Jack Ketch on their right, their coffins in their front, to Kennington Common; and who, in sight of the fire which was to consume their hearts, in sight of the quartering-block, in sight of the reeking entrails of their comrades, who had gone before, cried out "God save King James!" and went up the ladder to the gallows, smiling, and kissing the white cockade. Think of the Highland Chieftain—for Sir Walter's Fergus McIvor was no ideal creation: he lived and died for him whom he deemed the True Prince—captured at Culloden, who, sentenced to worse than a felon's death, smote his fettered hand on the ledge of the dock at Carlisle, and thus bespoke the judge: "Had I a hundred lives, my lord, I had perilled them all in this quarrel." Loyalty dreads no ignominious punishment, since, by loyalty, ignominy itself is annihilated. Still, I should like to know the names of those two Breton peasants who had learnt to play the light-infantry bugle. Mere clodhoppers they were, I have no doubt; munchers of black bread and garlic; benighted and bigoted frequenters of Pardons of Ploërmel and other superstitious mummeries, perchance; but a kind of Plutarch's Men, for all that.

The volatile, thoughtless, impracticable, but heroic widow of the Duc de Berri, showed that she herself did not shrink from danger. She determined to enter Nantes, and to go in the dress of a peasant girl. She was attended only by a Mademoiselle de Kersabiec, who also assumed the dress of a *paysanne*, and by M. de Ménars, who was disguised as a farmer. They had fifteen miles to travel. This was on the 16th of June, 1832. After an hour's pedestrianism, the clumsy hobnailed shoes and coarse woollen stockings worn by the Duchess so galled her delicate little feet that she philosophically pulled off her hose and shoes; put them into the large pocket of her linsey petticoat; and, like an Irish "colleen" going to mass, continued her march barefooted. Thus triumphantly did this Bourbon of the Bourbons give the lie to the pedantic gentleman-usher's aphorism about Feminine Royalty having no Legs.

Anon she reflected that the aristocratic whiteness of her lower limbs might betray her; so she picked up a handful of mud, and stained her symmetrical supports therewith. Nantes was reached at last, and the Duchess put on her shoes and stockings. After crossing the Pont Pyrmile, she found herself in the midst of a detachment of troops, commanded by an officer of the ex-body-guard of Charles X., whose face was perfectly familiar to her. She passed, however, unrecognised—perchance the ex-Garde du Corps did not care about recognising her—when, in the Place du Rouffai, somebody tapped her on the shoulder. It was an old apple woman who had placed her basket of fruit on the ground, and was unable to replace it on her head. "My good girls," she said, addressing the Duchess and Mademoiselle de Kersabicc, "help me, pray, to pick up my basket, and I will give each of you an apple." Marie Caroline immediately seized one handle of the pannier; made a sign to her companion to take the other; and the burden was speedily placed in equilibrium on the old woman's head, who—such is the way of the world—was going away without bestowing the promised guerdon, when the Duchess caught her by the arm, exclaiming, "Eh! la mère, ou est ma pomme?" She got her apple, and while she was munching it read very placidly a proclamation, signed by the Ministers of the Interior and of War, placing four departments of La Vendée in a state of siege, besides setting a heavy price on her own head. Not caring to trust herself just then to the tender mercies of Louis Philippe —who was bound to take care of her in the end, nevertheless—the Duchess consented, much against the grain, to go into hiding. An asylum was found for her at the house of a Legitimist lady named Deguigny, and there she doffed her peasant garments, which were long, and may be still, for aught I know, preserved as relics. The Legitimist lady hid her guest in a garret on the third floor, having a "priest's hole," so to speak, in case of need: being a recess within an angle formed by a chimney. An iron plate at the back of the grate was the entrance to the hiding-place, and was opened by a spring. In the wretched top room Marie Caroline remained until the month of October, desperately *ennuyée*, but occasionally manifesting signs of her unconquerable vivacity. She and M. de Ménars—that good and faithful servant, to whom surely it has been said "Well done"—absolutely re-papered the garret, covering it with a gay and flowery pattern devised between them. Was the art of flower-painting in water-colours ever pursued under more curious circumstances, I wonder?

The Duchesse de Berri was betrayed—betrayed by a horrible German Jew apostate named Simon Deutz, to whom she had stood sponsor on his "conversion" to Christianity, to whom she had been exceedingly kind, and who had been recommended to her by Pope Gregory XVI. as a person that she could safely trust. This Judas wormed himself into her secrets, and was her go-between and confidential man. Then the Beast went to the Ministry of the Interior, and sold the secret of his benefactress's hiding-place to M. Adolphe Thiers, for a huge sum of money. There is a story that the infamous bargain was struck on a dark and stormy night in the Champs Elysées

—little Monsieur Thiers, wrapped in a very large cloak, leaning against a tree; while Deutz whispered into his greedy but disgusted ear the fatal address, "Numero Trois, Rue-Neuve du Château, Nantes." There was a report also that the Beast had demanded, in addition to the blood-money, the Cross of the Legion of Honour; but at that request the conscience of M. Thiers stuck. It is somewhat consolatory to learn that prior to joining the Iscariot family, *là bas*, Simon Deutz took to imbibing brandy; was drunk night and day in the hovel he occupied at Belleville, where the *chiffonniers*, when they met him, used to spit at him; and that he died intoxicated, in horrible agonies.

M. Thiers, at all events, had obtained the precious address; and an honest, brave old

General, Dermoncourt by name, was ordered to surround the house in the Rue-Neuve du Château with a strong body of troops. The fugitives, MM. de Ménars and de Guibourg, and Mademoiselle de Kersabiec, had barely time to enter the "priest's hole." The Duchess was the last to conceal herself, observing with a smile, when her companions offered her precedence, that in a retreat "le général est toujours le dernier." She was in the act of closing the iron plate of the chimney when the soldiers entered the room. Now, Deutz did not know of the existence of this hole; and for many hours soldiers, gendarmes, police-spies, architects, and masons were all baffled. The search was protracted until a late hour in the night; and then General Dermoncourt and the Prefect of the Department went away; taking care, however, to leave sentries in every room of the mansion. Two gendarmes were placed on guard in the room where there was the recess behind the chimney. Meanwhile the luckless prisoners had remained perfectly still in a small closet only three feet and a half long, and eighteen inches wide at one extremity, but diminishing gradually to eight or ten inches at the other. In this exiguous slice of space they suffered frightful tortures; the gentlemen in particular, (being much taller than the two ladies), had scarcely room to stand upright, even by placing their heads between the rafters. The Duchess never complained. At dead of night the cold was so piercing that the gendarmes stationed in the room could hold out no longer. One of them went downstairs and returned with some dried turf; and in ten minutes a beautiful fire was burning on the hearth. At first the prisoners, who were half frozen in their concealment, hailed the change of temperature as a boon; but it grew hotter and hotter, and the wall itself became so charged with caloric that they shrank from touching it. The iron chimney-plate was tending towards a red heat. Meanwhile the gendarmes recommenced their search, and began to batter at the walls and ceiling with pickaxes and crowbars. The noise nearly deafened the poor little half-roasted Duchess; yet so unconquerable was her gaiety that she could not help laughing at the barrack-room jests of the policemen. Surely the names of these two gendarmes should have been preserved. Were they, we wonder, ever heard of afterwards at the Bouffes Parisiennes, or at the Philharmonic Theatre, Islington, marching and counter-marching to the portentous *refrain* of "We'll run 'em in"?

They ran the unlucky Duchess and her companions "in," or rather "out," at last. The prisoners enjoyed a short surcease from their torture when, the gendarmes going to sleep, towards five in the morning, the fire burnt low and the chimney-plate grew cool. But direr agony awaited them. One of the police-agents woke up, and proceeded to feed the flickering fire with a quantity of old numbers of *La Quotidienne*, which happened to be in the garret.

Imagine, under slightly parallel circumstances, Miss Nellie Farren and Mr. Lionel Brough concealed behind a pasteboard chimney-plate, and Mr. Toole, as a comic gendarme, blowing a pair of bellows on a canvas hearth. How the audience at the Gaiety Theatre would roar with laughter at this excruciatingly funny "situation." Now turn to the scene of agony and horror in the garret at Nantes.

The fumes from the burning paper penetrated through the chinks of the wall of the chimney, and all but suffocated the Duchess and her friends. Again the iron plate grew redhot. Twice the Duchess's dress caught fire; and she burnt her hands sorely in crushing out the flame. In her agitation she pushed back the spring which closed the door of the recess, and the iron chimney-panel gaped a little. Mademoiselle de Kersabiec immediately stretched forth her hand to close the aperture; but a turf sod, rolling back as the plate moved, attracted the notice of one of the gendarmes.

The honest fellow—he *must* have been attached to "Golo's army" — fancied that there were rats in the wall of the chimney. He awoke his comrade; and the pair placed themselves with drawn sabres on either side of the hearth, waiting to cut down the first rat that appeared. The Duchess by this time was in extremity, half choked, half roasted, and her dress again ablaze. M. de Ménars at last received a sign from the fainting lady, and kicked open the accursed iron plate. "Qui vive?" yelled the gendarmes, starting back in affright. "C'est Moi," was the reply, as the Captive strode over the blazing hearth. "Je suis la Duchesse de Berri." She was every inch a Duchess, and should have been every inch a Queen. She and her leal henchmen, and the young Vendean lady, had been in this hole, without food or light, for sixteen hours.

The conclusion of the Duchesse de Berri's Life-story belongs not to Romance, but to History of the plainest and, in some respects, of the unpleasantest nature. I am not, fortunately, called upon to relate it here. The Heroine's captivity in the Castle of Blaye, and its attendant circumstances, reflect infinite discredit, less politically than personally, on Louis Philippe, who used his fair and brave, though erring, kinswoman, in the scurviest and shabbiest manner possible. It does not matter now. *Sans de grands oublis la vie est impossible.* Louis Philippe sleeps, hard by Claremont; Marie Caroline in the vault of the Capuchins' Church at Goritz; and Fusion and Reconciliation reign among their descendants. Yet will posterity have something to say for the Mother who valiantly upheld her Son's rights. Those thousands of swords which Burke invoked were, alas! never drawn from their scabbards to avenge the wrongs of Marie Antoinette; but in times to come, when the Story of the Comte de Chambord and his Mother is related by abler pens than mine, there will surely arise among the nations a cry of "Brava! Bravissima! Maria Carolina!"

SPIERS & POND.
Christmas and Presentation Bin Cases.

SPIERS & POND beg to call attention to their special arrangements for the

CHRISTMAS SEASON,

during which the following cases of Wines and Spirits will be always ready at their Central Wine Depot, New Bridge Street, Ludgate, E.C., London.

Small Case (A), price Fifteen Shillings. Contains Half-dozen, comprising bottle each of excellent Port, Sherry, Brandy, Whiskey, Rum, and Gin.

Large Case (A), price Thirty Shillings. Contains One Dozen, comprising two bottles each of excellent Port, Sherry, Brandy, Whiskey, Rum, and Gin.

Small Case (C), price Eighteen Shilings and Sixpence. Contains Half-dozen, comprising a bottle each of selected Port, Sherry, Brandy, Whiskey, Rum, and Gin of superior quality.

Large Case (C), price Thirty-seven Shillings. Contain One Dozen, comprising two bottles each of selected Port, Sherry, Brandy, Whiskey, Rum, and Gin of superior quality.

All the above prices include Bottles and Cases.

The Christmas Cases contain Wines and Spirits of guaranteed excellence and purity. Orders to be accompanied by Remittances, and definite Instructions as to which Case shall be supplied, when it will be immediately forwarded free to any Metropolitan Railway Station, or to any address within the four mile radius.

Other Cases containing any kinds of Wines, Spirits, or Liqueurs, as selected by purchasers, will be forwarded to order at the shortest notice.

Wine List free on application or by Post. The Pro Rata Principle.

THE MIDLAND GRAND HOTEL,

St. Pancras Station, N.W.

Conducted by R. ETZENSBERGER,

Of the Hotel Victoria, Venice.

This Hotel offers to visitors all the advantages of the best known establishments in London. Luxury, Comfort, and Economy are here combined.

There is easy Railway communication from the Hotel to every part of the Metropolis.

THE MIDLAND GRAND HOTEL

Is the favourite resort of Tourists from all parts of the world.

ROBERT ETZENSBERGER, Manager.

GEORGE ROUTLEDGE & SONS' RAILWAY CATALOGUE.

⁎ *The columns of prices show the forms in which the Books are kept —e.g., Ainsworth's Novels are kept only in paper covers at 1/, or limp cloth gilt, 1/6; Armstrong's only in picture boards at 2/, or half roan 2/6.*

Paper Covers.	Limp Cl. Gilt.		Picture Boards.	Hf. Roan.
		AINSWORTH, W. Harrison—		
1/	1/6	Auriol	—	—
1/	1/6	Crichton	—	—
1/	1/6	Flitch of Bacon	—	—
1/	1/6	Guy Fawkes	—	—
1/	1/6	Jack Sheppard	—	—
1/	1/6	James the Second	—	—
1/	1/6	Lancashire Witches	—	—
1/	1/6	Mervyn Clitheroe	—	—
1/	1/6	Miser's Daughter...	—	—
1/	1/6	Old St. Paul's	—	—
1/	1/6	Ovingdean Grange	—	—
1/	1/6	Rookwood...	—	—
1/	1/6	Spendthrift	—	—
1/	1/6	Star Chamber	—	—
1/	1/6	St. James'	—	—
1/	1/6	Tower of London	—	—
1/	1/6	Windsor Castle	—	—

Ainsworth's Novels, in 17 vols., paper covers, price 17s.; cloth gilt, £1 5s. 6d.; 8 vols., half roan, £1 5s.

ALCOTT, Louisa M.—

1/	2/	Little Women	—	—
1/	2/	Little Women Married	—	—
1/	1/6	Moods	—	—

ARMSTRONG, F. C.—

—	—	Medora	2/	2/6
—	—	The Two Midshipmen	2/	2/6
—	—	War Hawk	2/	2/6
—	—	Young Commodore	2/	2/6

The Set, in 4 vols., cloth, 10s.; or boards, 8s.

Paper Covers.	Limp Cl. Gilt.		Picture Boards.	
		ARTHUR, T. S.—		
1/	1/6	Nothing but Money	—	—
		AUSTEN, Jane—		Cloth.
1/	1/6	Emma	—	2/
1/	1/6	Mansfield Park	—	2/
1/	1/6	Northanger Abbey and Persuasion	—	2/
1/	1/6	Pride and Prejudice	—	2/
1/	1/6	Sense and Sensibility	—	2/

Jane Austen's Novels, 5 vols., paper covers, 5s.; cloth, 7s. 6d.; Superior Edition, cloth, in a box, 10s.

		BALZAC—		
1/	—	Balthazar	—	—
1/	—	Eugenie Grandet	—	—
		BANIM, John—		Hf. Roan.
—	—	Peep o' Day	2/	2/6
—	—	Smuggler	2/	2/6
		BARHAM, R. H.—		
1/	—	My Cousin Nicholas	—	—
		BAYLY, T. Haynes—		
1/	1/6	Kindness in Women	—	—
		BELL, M. M.—		
—	—	Deeds, not Words	2/	2/6
—	—	The Ladder of Gold	2/	2/6
—	—	The Secret of a Life	2/	2/6
		BIRD, Robert M.—		
—	—	Nick of the Woods; or, The Fighting Quaker	2/	—
		BRET HARTE—		
		See "AMERICAN LIBRARY," page 23.		
		BROTHERTON, Mrs.—		
1/	1/6	Respectable Sinners	—	—
		BRUNTON, Mrs.—		
1/	—	Discipline	—	—
1/	—	Self Control	—	—
		BURY, Lady Charlotte—		
1/	—	The Divorced	—	—
1/	—	Love	—	—

Paper Covers.	Limp Cl. Gilt.		Picture Boards.	Hf. Roan.
		CARLETON, William—		
1/	1/6	Clarionet, &c.	—	—
1/	1/6	Emigrants	—	—
1/	1/6	Fardarougha the Miser	—	—
1/	1/6	Jane Sinclair, &c.	—	—
1/	1/6	Tithe Proctor	—	—

Carleton's Novels, 5 vols., paper covers, 5s.; cloth, 7s. 6d.

		CHAMIER, Captain—		
—	—	Ben Brace	2/	2/6
—	—	Jack Adams	2/	2/6
—	—	Life of a Sailor	2/	2/6
—	—	Tom Bowling	2/	2/6

Chamier's Novels, 4 vols., bds., 8s.; cloth, 10s.

		CLARKE, M. C.—		
—	—	The Iron Cousin	2/	—

		COCKTON, Henry—		
—	—	George Julian, the Prince	2/	2/6
—	—	Stanley Thorn	2/	2/6
—	—	Valentine Vox, the Ventriloquist	2/	2/6

Cockton's Novels, 3 vols., boards, 6s.; half roan, 7s. 6d.

		COLLINS, Charles Alston—		
—	—	A Cruise upon Wheels	2/	—

COOPER, J. Fenimore—

(SIXPENNY EDITION *on page* 20.)

Paper Covers.	Limp Cl. Gilt.		Cl. Boards Gilt, with Frontispiece.	
1/	1/6	Afloat and Ashore; a Sequel to Miles Wallingford	2/	2/6
1/	1/6	Borderers; or, The Heathcotes	2/	2/6
1/	1/6	Bravo; a Tale of Venice	2/	2/6
1/	1/6	Deerslayer; or, The First War-Path	2/	2/6
1/	1/6	Eve Effingham: A Sequel to "Homeward Bound"	—	—
1/	1/6	Headsman	2/	2/6
1/	1/6	Heidenmauer: a Legend of the Rhine	2/	2/6
1/	1/6	Homeward Bound; or, The Chase	2/	2/6
1/	1/6	Last of the Mohicans	2/	2/6
1/	1/6	Lionel Lincoln; or, The Leaguer of Boston	2/	2/6
1/	1/6	Mark's Reef; or, The Crater	—	—

Paper Covers.	Limp Cl. Gilt.		Picture Boards.	Cl Gilt, with Frontispiece.
		COOPER, J. FENIMORE—*continued.*		
1/	1/6	Miles Wallingford; or, Lucy Hardinge	2/	2/6
1/	1/6	Ned Myers; or, Life before the Mast	—	—
1/	1/6	Oak Openings; or, The Beehunter	—	
1/	1/6	Pathfinder; or, The Inland Sea	2/	2/6
1/	1/6	Pilot: a Tale of the Sea	2/	2/6
1/	1/6	Pioneers; or, The Sources of the Susquehanna	2/	2/6
1/	1/6	Prairie	2/	2/6
1/	1/6	Precaution	—	—
1/	1/6	Red Rover	2/	2/6
1/	1/6	Satanstoe; or, The Littlepage Manuscripts	—	—
1/	1/6	Sea Lions; or, The Lost Sealers	—	—
1/	1/6	Spy: a Tale of the Neutral Ground	2/	2/6
1/	1/6	Two Admirals	—	—
1/	1/6	Waterwitch; or, The Skimmer of the Seas	2/	2/6
1/	1/6	Wyandotte; or, The Hutted Knoll	2/	2/6

Cooper's Novels.—The Set of 18 vols., green cloth, £2 5s.; boards, £1 16s.

The SHILLING EDITION, 26 vols. in 13, cloth, £1 19s. Also 26 vols., cloth gilt, £1 19s.; paper covers, £1 6s.

See also page 20.

				Hf. Roan.
		COOPER, Thomas—		
1/	1/6	The Family Feud	—	—
		COSTELLO, Dudley—		
—	—	Faint Heart ne'er Won Fair Lady	2/	—
—	—	The Millionaire of Mincing Lane	2/	—
		CROLY, Rev. Dr.—		
—	—	Salathiel	2/	2/6
		CROWE, Catherine—		
—	—	Lilly Dawson	2/	2/6
—	—	Linny Lockwood	2/	2/6
—	—	Night Side of Nature	2/	2/6
—	—	Susan Hopley	2/	2/6

The Set, 4 vols., cloth, 10s.

NOVELS AT ONE SHILLING.

BY CAPTAIN MARRYAT.

Peter Simple.	Newton Forster.	The Phantom Ship.
The King's Own.	Jacob Faithful.	Percival Keene.
Midshipman Easy.	Japhet in Search of a Father.	Valerie.
Rattlin the Reefer.		Frank Mildmay.
The Pacha of Many Tales.	The Dog-Fiend.	Olla Podrida.
	The Poacher.	Monsieur Violet.

BY J. FENIMORE COOPER.

The Spy.	The Two Admirals.	The Sea Lions.
The Deerslayer.	The Red Rover.	Ned Myers.
The Waterwitch.	The Headsman.	

BY ALEXANDRE DUMAS.

The Three Musketeers.	Nanon; or, Woman's War.
Twenty Years After.	The Two Dianas.
Doctor Basilius.	The Black Tulip.
The Twin Captains.	The Forty-Five Guardsmen.
Captain Paul.	Taking the Bastile. 2 vols.
Memoirs of a Physician. 2 vols.	Chicot the Jester.
The Queen's Necklace.	The Conspirators.
The Chevalier de Maison Rouge.	Ascanio.
The Countess de Charny.	The Page of the Duke of Savoy.
Monte Cristo. 2 vols.	Isabel of Bavaria.

BY W. H. AINSWORTH.

Windsor Castle.	Guy Fawkes.	Lancashire Witches.
Tower of London.	The Spendthrift.	Ovingdean Grange.
The Miser's Daughter.	James the Second.	St. James's.
Rookwood.	The Star Chamber.	Auriol.
Old St. Paul's.	The Flitch of Bacon.	Jack Sheppard.
Crichton.	Mervyn Clitheroe.	

BY JANE AUSTEN.

Northanger Abbey.	Pride and Prejudice.	Mansfield Park.
Emma.	Sense and Sensibility.	

BY WILLIAM CARLETON.

Jane Sinclair.	Fardorougha.	The Tithe Proctor.
The Clarionet.	The Emigrants.	

BY GERALD GRIFFIN.

The Munster Festivals	The Rivals.	The Colleen Bawn.

Published by George Routledge and Sons.

Novels at One Shilling.—*Continued.*

By Maria Edgeworth.

Ennui.	Vivian.	The Absentee.	Manœuvring

American Humour.

The Celebrated Jumping Frog. *Mark Twain.*	The Hoosier Schoolmaster. *Edward Eggleston*
The Luck of Roaring Camp. *Bret Harte.*	Roughing It. *Mark Twain*
	The Innocents at Home. *Mark Twain*
Truthful James; and other Poems *Bret Harte.*	Maum Guinea. *M. A. Victor*

By Arthur Sketchley.

The Brown Papers.	Mrs. Brown in the Highlands.
Ditto. Second Series.	Mrs. Brown in London.
Mrs. Brown at the Sea-side.	Mrs. Brown on the Grand Tour
Mrs. Brown in America.	Mrs. Brown's Olliday Outins.
Mrs. Brown at the Play.	Mrs. Brown on the Alabama Claims.
Mrs. Brown on the Battle of Dorking.	Mrs. Brown at the International Exhibition.
Mrs. Brown on the Tichborne Case.	Miss Tomkins' Intended.
Mrs. Brown's Visits to Paris.	Out for a Holiday.

By Mrs. Gore.

The Royal Favourite.	The Ambassador's Wife.

By Nathaniel Hawthorne.

The Scarlet Letter.	The House of the Seven Gables

By Various Authors.

Violet the Danseuse.	Moods. *Louisa M. Alcott*
Joe Wilson's Ghost. *Banim.*	Kindness in Women.
The Old Commodore. *Author of "Rattlin the Reefer."*	Stories of Waterloo.
	My Brother's Wife.
Cinq Mars. *De Vigny.*	Tom Jones.
Ladder of Life. *A. B. Edwards.*	The Vicar of Wakefield.
Respectable Sinners.	A Seaside Sensation. *C. Ross*
Henpecked Husband. *Lady Scott.*	A Week with Mossoo. *Chas. Ross*
Nothing but Money. *T. S. Arthur.*	Love Tales. *G. H. Kingsley*
	Turf Frauds.
Letter-Bag of the Great Western. *Sam Slick.*	Nicholas's Notes.
	Sterne's Works.
The Family Feud. *Thos. Cooper.*	The Tichborne Romance.

Published by George Routledge and Sons.

CPSIA information can be obtained at www.ICGtesting.com
Printed in the USA
LVOW021159150213

320221LV00006BA/644/P